Words of Wisdom . . .

Thoughts of Hope

A collection of
poetry and meditations
to bless the heart and soul

ଔଷୠ

Mary Kay Glunt

Poetry and meditations in this book are the original
work of the author and are under copyright.
No part of this book may be reproduced or used in
any way without the express permission of Mary Kay Glunt.

Unless noted otherwise, illustrations are under copyright
restrictions and have been reproduced with permission.
Illustrations may not be copied, reproduced, or used without
express permission of the owner of the illustration, as noted.
Sources of illustrations can be found in List of Illustrations at back.

Unless specified otherwise, Bible verses quoted from the New
International Version, ©1985, The Zondervan Corporation

Words of Wisdom . . . Thoughts of Hope
by Mary Kay Glunt, ©2016
ISBN-13: 978-1534987753

Dedication

This collection is dedicated to all those who have been friends and mentors in the faith, to those who have encouraged me in ministry, and to those who have been faithful friends and family.

I am especially thankful to my husband, Don, who serves as my sounding board and advisor and helps me sort through my thoughts.

Finally, I dedicate this collection to my Lord and Savior, Jesus Christ, who never lets me go and who is making me into someone who can glorify God.

Preface

Verbal expression has always been an important part of my life (my brother said I talked too much!), and I love to rhyme. Writing prose and poetry gives me an outlet for my deepest thoughts and feelings and helps me as I develop my views on life. God's presence has given life to these words and thoughts, and likewise, the Holy Spirit speaking through these words has encouraged many.

This collection of writings includes poems written for friends and acquaintances, for people I knew well, and for some I didn't know at all, but each piece was written with prayer and faith in God's grace and love.

As you explore this collection, I hope you'll take the time to let the words resonate with your thoughts and needs. Enjoy the photos and illustrations. Contemplate the Bible passages. Let the Spirit speak to your heart and lift you up in God's loving arms.

I'm praying for each of you that God's Spirit will be present with you to bring you joy, peace, hope, and strength for your life.

Blessings!
Mary Kay Glunt

Table of Contents

Meditation / Poem

Chapter 1--Starting Points
- Who Are You? / Servant Prayer
- Finding Grace / A Soldier, Me?
- Simple Faith / Back-Door Chimes

Chapter 2--In the Midst of Life
- To Worry or Not to Worry? / Anxious Moments
- A God's Eye View / Work in Progress
- Grief Shaped By Hope / The Gift that Waits
- Joy in the Journey / Tribute to My Mother

Chapter 3—All in the Family of God
- How Can We See God? / Shining Bright
- Are We Related? / Sisters by Faith
- It Takes All Kinds / For My Child's First Teacher

Chapter 4--Testimonies of the Ages
- A Cloud of Witnesses / Carry On
- Freedom Isn't Free / I Remember You
- Hands of Love / The Golden Ring
- Generation to Generation / The Angel in My Grandma's House

Chapter 5—On the Way Home
- The Beauty of Adoption / From the Father's Heart
- Help for the Weary / Thank You, Lord, for Wings
- Following the Shepherd / Shepherd's Song
- On the Journey / Home!

List of Illustrations

Chapter 1

Starting Points

Who Are You?

How do you define yourself? By your family heritage? Maybe your academic pursuits make up your reason-for-being. Or maybe your career accomplishments are most important to your idea of who you are.

"Who am I?" is the question of the ages. Children ask their parents. Maybe who they are can be found in their lineage. Likewise, adopted children often initiate a search, hoping that the identity of their birth parents will reveal the answer. Teenagers seek assurance from their friends, hoping to find meaning in who their friends think they are. Adults seek meaning in their work and achievements or in the opinions of their counselors.

Who I am in Christ is the most basic level of this conundrum. So who am I? I am a child who was lost in sin, orphaned and separated from God because of my own sinfulness, but I was brought near, reunited with God, through the love of God in Christ. I am now a member of God's family because of the sacrifice of Jesus. I can be confident in that relationship. I am a child of God, loved and forgiven.

Yet, although I know and accept this truth mentally, I still struggle with the meaning of my life. In the "search for me" my first temptation is to discount my significance in this family, in this body of Christ, to diminish who I am and what God has called me to be. Looking at the abilities and gifts I have received from God, I consider them much less important or necessary to all that God is doing in this world. Similarly, I might be tempted to consider my gifts or talents more important than others in the body, a sense of grandiosity that is uncalled for.

How do I properly determine my value and purpose in God's economy? Does my contribution matter at all? Paul talks about this in 1 Corinthians: "If the foot should say, "Because I am not a hand, I do not belong to the body," it would not for that reason cease to be part of the body. And if the ear should say, "Because I am not an eye, I do not belong to the body," it would not for that reason cease to be part of the body" (12:15-16).

The flip side of this attitude is spiritual pride—"the work cannot be done without me." Paul continues: "The eye cannot say to the hand, 'I don't need you!' And the head cannot say to the feet, 'I don't need you!' On the contrary, those parts of the body that seem to be weaker are indispensable" (1 Corinthians 12:21-22).

Determining who I am requires one thing: to know Christ and the value God places on each of us—none greater and none lesser. God loves and gifts us all equally for the purpose of glorifying God and being God's ambassadors in this fallen world.

I've discovered who I am . . . Who are you?

> "How great is the love the Father has lavished on us, that we should be called children of God! And that is what we are! The reason the world does not know us is that it did not know him. Dear friends, now we are children of God, and what we will be has not yet been made known. But we know that when he appears, we shall be like him, for we shall see him as he is. Everyone who has this hope in him purifies himself, just as he is pure." 1 John 3:1-3

☙❧

Original source of photo unknown

Servant Prayer

*Your child, your own, adopted in,
no longer lost, astray;
blessed with all your righteousness
and strength to meet each day.*

*A life to live, a love to give,
all things you've given me.
I'm just a child who's been called in
to learn at Father's knee.*

*I learn, I grow, I fall behind.
I sometimes miss your call.
but you, my God, are always there
to catch me when I fall.*

*I'm just a child, and yet much more,
a servant made by you,
to show your love to all I meet
so they can know you too.*

*Oh may my heart be tender still
many years from now.
May I have served you faithfully
until my life's last bow.*

*It wasn't mine to ask or claim
until you sent your Son.
And now I ask, my God, send me
until your work is done.*

© 1989

*Written for a friend graduating from seminary
and going on to be a female paratrooper
chaplain in the U.S. Army.*

Finding Grace

As a little girl I loved to go to church. I'd sing at the top of my lungs (much to my siblings' chagrin) and recite the liturgy prayers by heart. I wanted to share the story of Jesus with others so they could love God, too. Most of all I loved to talk to God in prayer. Whether walking home from church, sitting alone in my bedroom, or sitting outside listening to the sounds of the city, I still remember some of those long-ago conversations between God and me.

Unfortunately, as I grew up and confronted the struggles of adolescence, like so many others, I moved away from that simple faith relationship with God. I no longer thought of myself as God's beloved daughter, but rather as a failure—someone who regularly disappointed God and others—and I constantly tried to make up for my weakness and sin in my own strength and by my own works. Unfortunately, that path only led to more failure, deeper feelings of shame, and despair.

Imagine my wonder and surprise when, at the age of 21, I sat with a young friend over coffee and heard, seemingly for the first time, the truth of God's grace and forgiveness. I finally realized that God's opinion of me didn't center around what I was able or unable to do for myself, but rather in God's plan made possible by Jesus' life, death, and resurrection. The burden of "have to be" was lifted! Even so, it has taken years for that truth to truly become a foundational part of my life.

What makes us try to "be" something special for God, to try to impress God with all that we can accomplish? Why do we feel we have to make up for what we have made of ourselves, instead of realizing that we are God's creation, that we are loved, cherished, and forgiven by God, in spite of what we were before? When will we learn that we are able to approach God only because of Jesus' sacrifice, not our own?

Looking back, it is obvious that as I grew older I began to depend on my own limited strength and abilities instead of depending on the mercy and grace of God. My task in live became a campaign to convince God that I could be acceptable. It has taken a long time to establish the habit, and now I remind myself—daily—that my value isn't found in what I do or how well I do it, or in what I have done right or wrong, but in the One in whom I believe. That makes all the difference.

> "Three times I pleaded with the Lord to take (the thorn in my flesh) away from me. But he said to me, "My grace is sufficient for you, for my power is made perfect in weakness." Therefore I will boast all the more gladly about my weaknesses, so that Christ's power may rest on me. That is why, for Christ's sake, I delight in weaknesses, in insults, in hardships, in persecutions, in difficulties. For when I am weak, then I am strong."
> (2 Corinthians 12:8-10)

> "For it is by grace you have been saved, through faith—and this is not from yourselves, it is the gift of God—not by works, so that no one can boast"
> (Ephesians 2:8,9)

ଓଃ଼ଓ

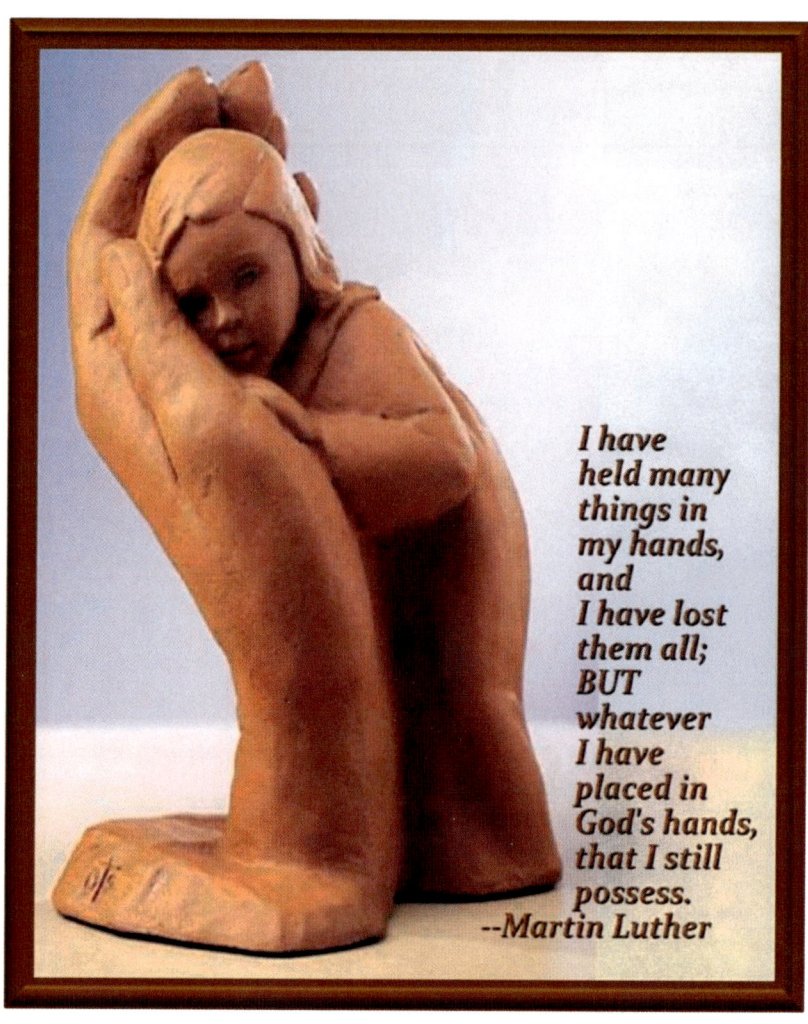

I have held many things in my hands, and I have lost them all; BUT whatever I have placed in God's hands, that I still possess.
--Martin Luther

A Soldier, Me?

"A soldier, me? My Lord," said he,
"my strength is very small."
"My child, it's not your strength I ask,
I only ask your all."

"A soldier, me? My Lord," said she,
"I have no sword to shine"
"My child, your sword would never do,
so I will give you mine."

"A soldier, me? My Lord," said he,
"No shield have I to hold."
"My child, behind the shield of faith
in Me you will be bold."

"A soldier, me? My Lord," said she,
"What cause shall I defend?"
"My child, the message of my Son,
His coming and the end."

"A soldier, me? My Lord," said he,
"I'll do as You command!"
"My child, the only thing I ask
is that you hold my hand.

©1989

Written for a friend's graduation from seminary; he had
been active military and was serving in the Reserves

Simple Faith

I was about ten years old, maybe nine, when I heard the "angels' songs." Alone in our row-house kitchen on a warm summer afternoon, I heard some kind of music through the window. Stepping out on the back door stoop, I looked around to find the source of the music. In the back of my mind I knew they were wind chimes, but there, in the alleyway between the houses, to me the sounds were divine, angels playing music in worship of God. Enraptured by the song of the chimes I stood there for several minutes, singing to God myself and enjoying God's presence there in my backyard.

Children have an awesome way of recognizing the miraculous and the beautiful in life. They see with different eyes and hear with different ears—senses that have yet to be tainted by the world's harshness. Children simply believe. Angels can play music to God, children can know God's presence, and beauty can be found even on the stoop of an inner-city row house.

> "At that time the disciples came to Jesus and asked, 'Who is the greatest in the kingdom of heaven?'
> "He called a little child and had him stand among them. And he said: 'I tell you the truth, unless you change and become like little children, you will never enter the kingdom of heaven. Therefore, whoever humbles himself like this child is the greatest in the kingdom of heaven'" (Matthew 18:1-4).

Here I sit in my back yard, over forty years later, listening to my wind chimes and remembering that beautiful experience, but today my mind is clouded by grown-up thoughts, experiences, and responsibilities. News reports daily tell about killings, thefts, and all-around selfishness. Recognizing the beauty of the "angels' song" is an intentional task now, regularly pushed out by everyday urgencies and problems.

Likewise, as we leave childhood behind, too often we remain "child-ish," exemplifying the worst of immaturity, selfishness, and greed. Most days we follow society's call by reverting to an attitude that everything belongs to and revolves around "ME"! Unfortunately, even though the majority of us act that way, it wasn't Jesus' intent that we act like children, but believe like children.

How can I be like a child and not be childish? What does Jesus want me to be if not "childish"? Note His words: "unless you change and become like little children." As Jesus held those children He was referring to their ability to believe, to love, and to give, to remember that God is in everything and that the miraculous is all around us.

No doubt you had an "angels' song" moment in your life, a time when the ordinary in life brought you to a place of awe and wonder at God's presence. Go back and remember the awe and rapture of that experience. Whatever your struggle today, remember that God is in the small things and the big things, and you can trust in God.

Back Door Chimes

Standing on my porch I long
to hear the strains of angels' songs,
with notes and pitch in perfect score
in worship to our gracious Lord.

But on my porch I hear of strife
and problems that bring grief to life.
I see around not just the lost,
but Christians who have paid the cost.

Here upon my porch I stand
and long to hear the angel band,
but grown-up thoughts and grown-up fears
all bring a deafness to my ears.

Once as a child at my back door
I heard the angels' songs adore.
The chiming of the notes that played
called to my heart in wondrous praise.

I couldn't see the hand that caused
the instrument to worship God.
I only heard the music sweet
that thrilled my all, from head to feet.

Enraptured there with childhood faith
I knew the angels sang and played,
although adults would say, "That's wind
playing songs on glass and tin."

As children's hearts are turned to God
by simple things, though weak or flawed,
songs by wind on glass and tin
can overcome the world's mean din.

Upon my porch I hear the chimes,
though man-made, still play songs divine.
I join in, first with feeble hum,
then lift my voice, "Lord Jesus, come,
and set us free from pain and grief
that buffet us without relief."
And in that prayer, that song inspired,
I find that faith has not retired.

From simple things,
like glass and tin,
hung in tandem
all with string,
in the midst of
grief and strife
and all the fears
and pain of life,
I hearken to
a simpler place
alone with God in
childlike faith,
and join the chimes
of glass and tin
to with the angels
worship Him.

©1993

Picture by Mary Kay Glunt, 2016

Chapter 2

In the Midst of Life

To Worry or Not to Worry? That Is the Question!

Hope—such a precious commodity. Anxiety—so prevalent, especially when you consider the general attitudes of anger, hatred, and lack of concern for others in our world today. No wonder many of us find ourselves worrying every day, but is it necessary?

The presence of doubt is different from entertaining anxiety. Consider the man whose son was possessed by an evil spirit. Knowing the enormity of the miracle he needed, he petitioned Jesus, "I do believe; help me overcome my unbelief" (Mark 9:24). God knows we will have doubts. In fact, when people truly wanted to believe, but found it hard to do so, Jesus gave them assurance and acknowledged the little faith they had.

Anxiety doesn't ask God for assurance, but rather attempts to resolve problems through worry. An unknown author once said, "Troubles are a lot like people—they grow bigger if you nurse them." While we shouldn't ignore our problems, the more we emphasize our troubles and fears, the more dominant our fears become, overshadowing our faith in God.

Chemical imbalances can cause anxiety, relieved only by medical treatment. However, absent such a condition, many anxieties are founded in this basic truth: I haven't truly settled in my mind and heart that God loves me, is with me, and will bring me through, no matter what my situation, surroundings, or my mind tell me. Armed with this truth, I can calm my racing heart, soothe my frazzled nerves, and defeat my anxieties through my reliance on and faith in Christ.

There are some small steps we can take to avoid anxiety's control. I can pray instead of complaining. When I'm anxious, or even a bit angry, I can take a deep breath and count to ten. An even better solution is to *reflect on a Bible verse that is meaningful to me! (Of course, that assumes I actually know a few Bible verses. That's another subject!) Can't think of one yourself? I suggest Philippians 4:19: "I can do all things through Christ who strengthens me."*

The author of Proverbs puts it this way: Trust in the Lord with all your heart and lean not on your own understanding, in all your ways submit to him, and he will make your paths straight" (vv. 5-6).

Believers don't ignore the world around us. We look through spiritual eyes with vision that comes through our faith in God. Trying to fight anxiety and worry? Turn your thoughts to the God who IS and who IS with you!

An anxious heart weighs a man down, but a kind word cheers him up (Proverbs 12:25).

Do not be anxious about anything, but in everything, by prayer and petition, with thanksgiving, present your requests to God (Philippians 4:6)

ଓଞ୍ଚ

"Give your entire attention to what God is doing right now, and don't get worked up about what may or may not happen tomorrow.

God will help you deal with whatever hard things come up when the time comes.

                Matthew 6:34, The Message

Photo by Don Glunt, ©2016
Used with permission

Anxious Moments

In my anxious moments—
  which are more than I care to admit—
    I tend to forget
      that my days are numbered,
      that my future is in Your hands.

The present becomes all that I own
  skewed by all that has been—
    in reality and in my perception.

Lord, help me to breathe deeply,
  letting Your breath bring
    peace and patience.

So often, as I am tempted to react,
  to defend, or to justify,
    help me, Lord, to sit deeply and exhale.

As the voices around me tease
  and draw me upward
    in emotion and frustration,
  help me to look up,
    and with uplifted hands and heart,
      to see the reason I am here—
      to reflect Your love to others
        in an anxious
          "can't-see-God" world.

@2000

A God's Eye View

"I want a keepsake poem for my friend"

"Tell me a little about her."

"She likes cross-stitch, and she goes to church."

Usually a person ordering a personalized poem gives me a bit more information about the recipient, but this time all I had to go on was "she likes cross-stitch and goes to church."

I struggled with this project. How could I create something meaningful for this woman, something that would inspire and celebrate her with so little to go on? Then I remembered a story told by Corrie ten Boom, the woman who called herself a "tramp for the Lord."

Corrie and her family lived in the Netherlands during World War II. Their faith "inspired them to serve society, offering shelter, food and money to those in need." This faith moved them to protect Jewish neighbors targeted by the Third Reich. They were successful for a time, but a neighbor turned them in, and they were arrested by the Gestapo and placed in prison camps.

Corrie and Betsie were placed in the Ravensbrück concentration camp where they suffered unimaginable indignities. Corrie's faith was tested, but she was inspired by her sister's deep faith and prayers for their captors. Betsie died in that camp, and Corrie was released days later because of a clerical error, one week before all women her age were killed.

While in the only member of her family to survive the Nazi death camps, Corrie learned the hard way that "we below the picture miss because we only see a trace." Walking away from that camp, a miracle in itself, Corrie could have been angry at God and others, but she chose to call on God in faith once again, and she became God's vessel to bring healing and hope to many. She traveled the world telling others about the *forgiving, restoring love of Jesus, even to former concentration camp guards.*

We don't know what picture will appear when today's joys or troubles are placed alongside our remaining life experiences. We don't know how God will use us in the lives of others. And when we are in midst of the valley, we just might find it hard to believe that God is still in control.

Consider Naomi, an Israelite woman living in a foreign country. She lost her husband and both of her sons to death. No one would blame her for being confused and angry. Yet, Naomi chose to go back to her home, to the place where she first found faith in God. And she brought her Moabite daughter-in-law Ruth with her. What a picture of faith and love!

If you haven't read the book of Ruth, I'll give away the ending. Ruth meets and marries Boaz (a relative of Naomi's husband), and they have a child named Obed (which means "servant"). Through that child Naomi becomes not only a grandmother, but an ancestor of our Lord Jesus Christ. Not a bad ending, and probably one she never saw coming!

> *"The women said to Naomi: 'Praise be to the Lord, who this day has not left you without a kinsman-redeemer. May he become famous throughout Israel! He will renew your life and sustain you in our old age. For your daughter-in-law, who loves you and who is better to you than seven sons, has given him birth.'" Ruth 4:14*

Additional reading: Corrie ten Boom wrote about her experience in her book, **The Hiding Place,** *and others.*

> Jesus replied,
> "You do not realize now
> what I am doing,
> but later you will
> understand."
> John 13:7

Sea Beside Seashore
Sabri Ismail

Work in Progress

Taking narrow lengths of string,
    many colors, many shades.
        Each one alone its message brings—
            the only star in its parade.

Armed with pattern, needle, floss,
    the stitcher starts to make a change
        to canvas woven "criss" and "cross,"
            colors, stitches all arranged.

Woven canvas, blank and plain,
    changes in the stitcher's hand—
        up one row and back again,
            each stitch and color just as planned.

Now a picture starts to show
    as colors mix and stitches blend
        with each new stitch the image grows
            but not complete until the end.

You see, our lives are much like this,
    experiences fill each space,
        and we below the picture miss
            because we only see a trace.

Above us God the picture sees
    as stitches empty squares replace.
        And God designed just what you'll be
            so rest in God's amazing grace.

©2004

Grief Shaped by Hope

There were many things left to do in the nursery, but he wasn't going to wait. The months of waiting were shortened when she went into labor two months early. The doctors tried to stop the contractions, but it wasn't to be, and a beautiful, perfect baby boy was born, albeit tiny and weak.

After two months of neonatal intensive care, he seemed to be responding. His kidneys were functioning on their own, and he had gained weight. It seemed as if he would finally be coming home when, all of a sudden, everything began to shut down. Within days the beautiful, tiny baby boy was no longer an object of hope and prayer, but just a memory and a reminder of their now empty arms.

Of all the things to grieve, the loss of a child may be one of the hardest, especially the loss of a newborn baby. The weeks of hope and joy, preparation and anticipation, are suddenly cut short by an often-times unexplainable turn of events, leaving an emptiness that cuts very deep into the hearts of the parents and family. The parents don't even have the memories of the first smile, first step, or first word to hold on to.

Grief takes many shapes and, whatever the loss, we will never "just get over it." We grieve for the unspoken words, the lost opportunities, the unfulfilled hopes. Even more, the grieving process is a natural, necessary part of recovering from loss. Just stoically moving on is unhealthy. We grieve because our attachment to the person, place, or thing is severed. The grieving process allows us to feel the pain of loss as we remember and honor what we have lost. This allows us to move on. We don't forget the object of our grief, but rather, eventually, we are able to remember it fondly, in spite of its absence.

Struggling with the death and absence of their loved ones, the believers in Thessalonica were grief-stricken. Paul wrote to them,

> "Brothers, we do not want you to be ignorant
> about those who fall asleep, or to grieve like
> the rest of men, who have no hope. We
> believe that Jesus died and rose again and so
> we believe that God will bring with Jesus
> those who have fallen asleep in him. . . . And
> so we will be with the Lord forever. Therefore
> encourage each other with these words"
> (1 Thessalonians 3:13, 14, 18)

When we think about the moments we have had, the joys we have experienced, and the future that awaits us, we can find hope and joy in the midst of our sorrow. Because I believe in God, I also believe there will be a tomorrow. And because I believe in God's promises, I know I will see my loved ones again. The gift is waiting. We press on and live for Christ, knowing that one day we will be reunited with God and with our loved ones. We hold on to God's promise because, as stated by the Apostle Paul, we know that "in all things God works for the good of those who love him, who have been called according to his purpose" (Romans 8:28).

But until the day we see our loved ones again, or until we see the fulfillment of what God is doing in our lives, we can know that we, too, are held, safely, in the loving arms of Jesus.

> "Be merciful to me, Lord, for I am in distress;
> my eyes grow weak with sorrow, my soul and
> body with grief. My life is consumed by anguish
> and my years by groaning; my strength fails
> because of my affliction, and my bones grow
> weak. But I trust in you, Lord; I say, "You are
> my God." . . . My times are in your hands; . . .
> Be strong and take heart,
> all you who hope in the Lord."
>
> Psalm 31:9-10, 14-15, 24

"In His Constant Care"
© Simon Dewey 2016

Permission Altus Fine Art/www.altusfineart.com

The Gift that Waits

A tiny hand, so very small;
a footprint like a baby doll;
Small ears, small eyes, and mouth below,
petite but perfect even though.

He wasn't what you thought you'd see,
a baby, yes, but small and weak.
Still you loved and cherished him,
and prayed through nights both bright and dim.

It wasn't long enough to see
him walk and talk and ride your knee.
But even though his time was short,
you knew his love, and he knew yours.

So now you walk, but not alone,
for Christ is with you as you go.
Look up because the gift's not gone
he's waiting in the Father's arms.

©2004

Written to comfort parents and grandparents on the loss of their infant son.

Joy in the Journey

As early as I can remember, Mom was the life of the party, full of laughter and activity. Even though she had multiple physical problems throughout the years, you could always count on "Aunt Mimi" to dance a polka or "cut a rug" with all the energy she could muster. She was always quick to help someone or to make them feel better when they were struggling. Wherever we went, people would fawn all over her. Once they met her, Mom was everybody's Aunt Mimi.

We said good-bye to Mom in May 2006. The many maladies, infections, and other problems had finally taken their toll, and we spent her last 24 hours in the hospital, reminiscing with her and celebrating the woman some of us knew as "Mom," some as "Aunt Mimi," and others, especially the nursing staff, as Mary with the big smile and sparkling green eyes.

What is it about laughter and hope that attracts us? Is it the comfort that comes from sharing in another's freedom and joy? Maybe it is the hope that comes from seeing someone else smile through their pain, helping us know that we can make it, too.

The apostle Paul wrote to the believers in Corinth about this very attitude.

> "For God, who said, "Let light shine out of darkness," made his light shine in our hearts to give us the light of the knowledge of the glory of God in the face of Christ. But we have this treasure in jars of clay to show that this all-surpassing power is from God and not from us. We are hard pressed on every side, but not crushed; perplexed, but not in despair; persecuted, but not abandoned; struck down, but not destroyed." (2 Corinthians 4:6-9)

Looking at our challenges according to "what we can handle" brings frustration and despair. It's hard to handle the perplexities and pain of life on our own. We feel as if we are destroyed when struggles occur. If we are relying on our own strength, the problems that press on us from every side will crush us.

The secret to the overcoming life, first of all, involves the belief that Christ died for me and dwells in my heart through the work of the Spirit of God.

Second, I need to recognize that I am not alone in this life. Because I belong to Christ, I am walking with One whose power is greater than any attack, any struggle, any pressure, the One who has specific plans for my life.

Third, I take encouragement from the victories and hope of those around me and thereby rekindle my own hope.

I believe Mom was able to help others release their frustrations, fears, and sorrows with her antics and fun because she knew there was so much more to life than her own pain and frustrations.

Mom, I owe you.

Thanks for the gift of laughter.

Jesus, I owe you.

Thanks for the gift of life!

In the Midst of Life

Our Mom and everybody's "Aunt Mimi"
Mary Baker Caristo
May 1, 1929 – May 31, 2006

We miss you, Mom

Tribute to My Mother

Many people say to me
  "Your laugh's so bright and full of glee."
    I tell them, "It's not mine, you see.
      My precious mom gave it to me."

Oh, please don't think her life sublime
  with fun and laughter all the time.
    She made ends meet, but there were times
      she had to count out every dime.

Though everything was not the best,
  with my mother we were blessed.
    She made sure we were fed and dressed
      and spread her cheer to every guest.

How did she smile and seem so glad
  even when she felt so bad,
    when it seemed she would explode,
      struggling under life's hard load?

Even so my mother laughed
  and danced and sometimes acted daft.
    For us she took her hurt and pain
      and gave it back with joy again.

Ready smile and hopeful dreams,
  laughing till I burst my seams,
    love of music, love of dance,
      these are my inheritance.

© 2004

Written for my mother's birthday.

Love Finds a Way

Life was exciting and fulfilling as DeDe cared for her patients. There really was very little time for much more, especially relationships. Miles away, Dana worked at his machine shop and raising his son, taking each day as it came. In each of their lives, however, there was so much more to come, but first came the diagnosis of multiple sclerosis. Each in their own lives heard the doctor, and each dealt with the disease's increasing disability on their own. They sought out strength through their faith in God and with their families, and then sought out support on the internet with an MS support group. A friendship forged, and over the years, their friendship became something more.

Who would have thought that something so terrible, a long-term disabling disease, could have brought about a tender, hopeful miracle? At each of their diagnoses, doctor appointments, and steps forward and back, the loneliness and fear was ever in the back of their minds; however, in the support group they found others with like diagnoses who understood their fears and their concerns, their pain and their losses. In this mix of laughter and tears Dana and DeDe found each other and married several years later.

Dana and DeDe are a true example of sacrificial love and commitment. Although Dana is in a motorized wheelchair, he refuses to give in to the disease. His love for DeDe is evident. And DeDe, well, in spite of her "diagnosis," she cares for Dana with a heart so big I can't imagine how it fits in her chest! Here in the Missouri hills, far from her home in Illinois, they have weathered the storms of life as their love for each other, and for God, has grown.

Things happen. We all wish we knew the future, but we don't. And when things happen—a failed marriage, the loss of a child or other family members, a devastating diagnosis—we are tempted to shake our fists and rail at God for not caring for us, for not answering our prayers. But, as is often the case, God is answering our

prayers, though not always the ones we speak out loud. In this case God gave them something they didn't even dare to pray for. In the face of a diagnosis that seemed to say their lives were over, God gave them to each other.

What are you facing today? Are you grieving a loss in your life and wondering why God isn't answering your prayers? God really is in control and thinking of you. You can be sure that you are not alone and that God has a plan. It may not be what you expected, but it will be good. After all, isn't that what faith is about, believing that somehow God has a plan?

It takes a decision of the will to believe God has something more for us, a daily—maybe even momentary—decision to believe that no matter what, the same God who holds the heavens and the earth holds my tiny life in his hands and loves me. Take a moment today to renew your relationship with the God who loves you. Give God the opportunity to grant the deepest wishes in your heart, even the ones you don't even dare speak. Then trust in God and wait on God's blessings.

> "As the deer pants for streams of water,
>   so my soul pants for you, my God.
>
> "My soul thirsts for God, for the living God.
>   When can I go and meet with God?
>
> "My tears have been my food day and night,
>   while people say to me all day long,
>   "Where is your God?"
>
> "Why, my soul, are you downcast?
>   Why so disturbed within me?
>   Put your hope in God,
>   for I will yet praise him,
>   my Savior and my God."
>
> Psalm 42:1-3, 5

His Eye Is on the Sparrow
Cindi Koeich
To Such as These Designs

The Gift of Love

*Love comes to every person
at least once in a lifetime.
It comes to them by Spirit's wind
and sacrifice sublime.*

*So rich the precious love of Christ
filling hearts within, but
sometimes miracles occur
and we are blessed again,
as suddenly and wondrously,
with joy and great surprise,
deep within two precious hearts
new hopes of love arise.*

*Often in this moment sweet
through Jesus' glorious grace,
unselfish love becomes their song,
the beauty on each face.*

*Grant, O Lord, their love today
will grow and deepen too,
so this, Your miracle of love
can testify to You.*

©2004

Chapter 3

All in the Family

How Can Others See God?

The Children of Israel, on their exodus from Egypt, had the tremendous experience of God's presence with them, seen in the pillar of fire at night and the pillar of cloud by day. These visual representations of God's care for them served to guard, protect, and lead them on their exodus from slavery and suffering in Egypt, as they journeyed to the Promised Land.

Unlike those days, we live in a world where it often takes a little more observation and sensitivity to detect God's presence with us. The trials and necessities of life demand so much of our attention that we don't recognize God's hand in all that is happening to us. We find ourselves wondering where God is when we need Him. Reflecting on this question will bring many answers, but one special beacon of God's presence is that which is found in the individual believer.

The apostle Paul saw God's presence in the believers who lived in Ephesus.

> "We always thank God, the Father of our Lord Jesus Christ, when we pray for you, because we have heard of your faith in Christ Jesus and of the love you have for all God's people" (Colossians 1:3-5).

The people of Colossae were people of faith. Paul had heard of their faithfulness to the teachings of the elders, but even more, Paul had heard of their expression of faith in love to those in the church. Not just a genteel greeting with spiritual overtones, their faith was expressed in love, a practical expression demonstrated by true concern for others in the community. As Paul taught the believers in Galatia, "For in Christ Jesus neither circumcision nor uncircumcision has any value. The only thing that counts is faith expressing itself through love" (Galatians 5:6).

How do others see your faith lived out? Do they see your kind glance and a pleasant, "God be with you"? Or do they experience your faith by your actions? When others recount your faith, how will they describe it: Flat and legalistic or active and living? Even a cursory reading of the book of James, it is clear that our expressions of faith must be more than just appearance or words. True faith is expressed in action, just as Jesus Christ physically gave His life for each of us.

"A new command I give you: Love one another. As I have loved you, so you must love one another. By this everyone will know that you are my disciples, if you love one another" (John 13:34-35).

We sing, "I love you with the love of the Lord." Yet, people won't know that we are disciples of Christ because of the songs we sing or the smiles we share. Jesus insisted that the way to represent God is to live as He lived, to love as He loved. This is the kind of love that acts, that supports, that moves into action when a need is revealed.

So what do people see when they observe our lives? Is our faith expressed in words alone? Or is our faith demonstrated with love and concern for our neighbors, from those closest to us to the least, from those who look like us to those who are very different?

When your epitaph is written, what will be written? Will it say, "a person who professed faith in Christ"? Or will it say, "a person who loved God by loving others"?

Shining Bright

It isn't in the rainbow that
God's glory's seen the best.
It isn't in the gemstone's fire,
its color or its zest.
God's glory isn't only known
through morning's welcome light
or recognized when sunlight fades
to twinkling starry night.

The seekers' eyes may see God's splendor
in creation's song,
In morning's light, in daytime bright,
in nighttime's brilliant throng.
But even when their eyes are blinded
to God's glory bright,
God's glory may always be seen
through friendship's loving sight.

In God's heart was born the gift
of mercy and of grace;
the gift was given to the earth
in Jesus' warm embrace.
fully God and fully human,
God's veiled mystery,
to walk with us, to welcome us
into God's family.

Jesus showed us through His life
and death God's perfect will:
to give himself, for love alone,
on Jerusalem's dark hill.
In darkness deep and grief untold
a light still brightly shone
as fallen earth could sing again,
no longer lost, alone.

*Each time a person gives his heart
to help without regard,
when she reaches out in love
to someone hurt and marred,
God's glory can be seen again
if only in small part,
helping all to know again
the greatness of God's heart.*

*So sing God's glory with your mouth,
in music deep and strong,
And speak of glory through your words
that tell of heaven's song.
But most of all let glory bright
flow out in all you do
BY loving others as Christ loved
and sacrificed for you.*

@2004

All the darkness in the world cannot extinguish the light of a single candle.

-Francis of Assisi

Are We Related?

Sorority sisters. Lodge brothers. The "sibling" idea encompasses more than relation by blood or lineage. Each group finds its own common points and then builds relationships around them.

Growing up in a primarily Eastern European neighborhood, with first- and second-generation Americans and even recent immigrants, family was truly an extended experience. There was always someone who knew you or a member of your family, wherever you wandered. And the relationships forged by our families when they arrived in America became a new basis for "family."

Beyond all of that, I was privileged to grow up in a family that, for the most part, kept us close. My cousins, on both sides, were friends with whom I spent most of my time, and to this day I count them as some of my best friends.

My cousin Kathy was an only child whose dad passed away when she was only 8 years old (I was 5). Because her mom had to work full-time, Kathy spent most of her time with us after school, and I spent a lot of time in their third-floor apartment. Kathy was my "mentor" when I entered high school, showing me the ropes and having her friends look out for me. We were sisters in the heartfelt meaning of the word.

Several years later, she asked about my recent "religious" experience. I had moved away, but when I returned a year later, many things were different. Sunday mornings were once again time for God, and my Bible actually made it off of my shelf! She wanted to know what had changed. As God often does, He turned around the relationship, allowing me to give back to Kathy by pouring out the beautiful experience of realizing God's love for me. Struggling for meaning and hope in her own life, she, too, asked Christ to forgive her sins and renew her.

What does it mean to be a brother or sister? It isn't just blood or family relations, and it goes much deeper than a fraternal membership. Paul tells us that when we are in Christ we are all brothers and sisters because

> *"You are all [children] of God through faith in Christ Jesus, for all of you who were baptized into Christ have clothed yourselves with Christ. There is neither Jew nor Greek, slave nor free, male nor female, for you are all one in Christ Jesus. If you belong to Christ, then you are Abraham's seed, and heirs according to the promise" (Galatians 3:26-29).*

The closest sibling relationship is nothing compared to the knowledge that we are brothers and sisters in Christ. Our family ties go way beyond blood or law, but to the very depths of our being, to the One who created each of us. In this way I am doubly blessed by those in my life who are related, not only by blood or affiliation, but also by faith in Christ.

> *"But when the set time had fully come, God sent his Son, born of a woman, born under the law, to redeem those under the law, that we might receive adoption to sonship. Because you are his sons [and daughters], God sent the Spirit of his Son into our hearts, the Spirit who calls out, 'Abba, Father.' So you are no longer a slave, but God's child; and since you are his child, God has made you also an heir."(Galatians 4:4-7).*

CR80

*Kathy, her mom, and me in earlier years
(her crown was always a little crooked!)*

> I did nothing to deserve God's love;
> in fact, I was living as an orphan
> without hope.
> Yet God chose to pursue
> a relationship with me.
> and through the death of his son, Jesus,
> I was adopted into God's family.
>   Steven Curtis Chapman

Sisters by Faith

We each have different mothers.
Our fathers aren't the same.
But still you're like a sister
in more than just the name.

We played when we were "kidlets"
and shared both fun and tears.
We learned to play all kinds of games
somewhere along the stairs.

Sometime in the middle
we called to God in faith,
asking for forgiveness and a
pass through heaven's gate.

Once again we bonded,
but this time sisters true,
as Christ then made us by His grace
His daughters fresh and new.

Now we're in the "grown-up" phase
with children, jobs, and homes.
But still in heart we're sisters
wherever we may roam.

© 2004

Written for Kathy's 50th birthday.

It Takes All Kinds

An old African proverb states, "It takes a whole village to raise a child." While we in the "civilized" West might bristle at the thought of someone else correcting our children, the truth is that very few children are raised without the influence, for good or bad, of the community at large. It takes all kinds of people, with all kinds of talents and many life examples to help a child reach maturity and adulthood.

Besides your parents, who were the people involved in your upbringing? Teachers, aunts, uncles, grandparents, and neighbors were probably purveyors of the learning you received. Think back on the examples they brought to you, both negative and positive, and how those examples helped to form the person you have become.

As you remember those who helped in your formation, I wonder how you are involved in the lives of people with whom you are in contact. The modern person often lives in a famine of relationships. Our days are too full of activity to build long-lasting, stable relationships with others in our lives, sometimes too full to build strong relationships even with our own children. We are taught to be independent , but then, because we are so strong, we sometimes fail to be responsible to others in our lives.

The "whole village" concept is much more than everyone being responsible for the children. It is an expression of faith and community that builds strong ties and relationships that can fill in the gap in the areas where we might fall short. As believers, we are responsible to one another, not to live as "islands," totally independent to the exclusion of others.

> "And we urge you, brothers and sisters, warn those who are idle and disruptive, encourage the disheartened, help the weak,

be patient with everyone. Make sure that nobody pays back wrong for wrong, but always strive to do what is good for each other and for everyone else."
(1 Thessalonians 5:14-15)

The writer of Ecclesiastes expressed it this way:

"Two are better than one, because they have a good return for their labor: If either of them falls down, one can help the other up. But pity anyone who falls and has no one to help them up. Also, if two lie down together, they will keep warm. But how can one keep warm alone? Though one may be overpowered, two can defend themselves. A cord of three strands is not quickly broken"
(Ecclesiastes 4:9-12).

To whom or to what are you tethered? Do you have others in your life that can pick you up when you fall down? Have you built strong relationships with others of like-minded faith? Do you pray for those around you, for their strength and growth in God?

When we each take our parts in the body of Christ, when we each contribute our individual gifts and receive the gifts of others, we will be partners, not only in the growth of our children, but also in our own growth, as we grow spiritually and emotionally to the completion of the work begun in each of us.

The one who calls you is faithful, and he will do it (1 Thessalonians 5:24).

ೞ✺ಲ

For My Child's First Teacher

*One day late in summer I brought my gift,
tender, shy, and full of wonder,
And there, with my heart full of hope and fear,
I left my little one in your care.*

*How could I leave God's precious gift
in the care of someone barely an acquaintance?
I was given the gift to train, to lead,
to be God's hand extended to a young life.*

*With a kiss, and a long hug,
on that late summer day,
I turned and walked away,
Praying for my child and praying for you.*

*God placed that blessing in my hand,
and I had done my best
to plant the seeds of knowledge, of faith, of wonder,
In a forming mind.*

*I prayed for you as I walked away,
because you had become my partner.
Not just a teacher, a caretaker, a sitter,
but my partner in knowledge and growth.*

*A year has passed, and through the days,
as he became more independent,
as she became more confident,
I walked away with a silent prayer.*

*"God bless this person whom you have called
to serve and train and love these children.
Give joy in this calling, and patience as well,
and bless this teacher for all that will be shared."*

*And now here we stand, on a day late in spring,
as summer's light is stealing in,
to say good-bye, to graduate,
my child, my little one, to a new experience.*

*You will always be my child's first teacher,
and you will always be in my heart,
as a teacher, as a mentor, and as a friend,
but most of all as a partner in raising God's gift to me.*

*Thank you for all you've done
and for all you continue to do
for our children.*

@ 2001

*Written for my children's first teachers,
this poem was our thank-you gift
for their investment in our children's lives.*

"Kindergarten" by Hugo Oehmichen (1843–1932)
The resolution isn't the greatest, but this I really liked this print.

Chapter 4

Testimonies of the Ages

A Cloud of Witnesses

> "Now faith is being sure of what we hope for and certain of what we do not see. This is what the ancients were commended for." (Hebrews 11:1).

Faith. Volumes have been written to define it, yet the author of Hebrews does so in one sentence. Expanding on this definition, he recites the history of the ancestors, revisiting their faith choices through the years. Following this historical retrospective, we hear this challenge:

> "Therefore, since we are surrounded by such a great cloud of witnesses, let us throw off everything that hinders and the sin that so easily entangles, and let us run with perseverance the race marked out for us" (12:1)

Like those living in parts of our world today, the early believers were often in danger of betrayal and/or punishment for their faith. Choices made and words spoken could make the difference between life and death for themselves and their families. However, as the author reminded them, our choices should be made not on the basis of fear of consequences, but on the basis of faith in God's promises.

History can be an amazing teacher and guide, especially when we find ourselves in times of challenge and doubt. We retell stories of those who lived before us, recite their accomplishments and failures, and take courage because of testimonies of how God moved in their lives. The eventuality of this truth is that we, then, become the ancestors, the "ones who have gone before," leaving behind the testimony of our experiences of faith for others.

One of my favorite songs, *Find Us Faithful*, by Steve Green, is about this truth. My prayer, as is his in the chorus, reads:

> "May all who come behind us find us faithful.
> May the fire of our devotion light their way.
> May the footprints that we leave
> lead them to believe
> And the lives we live inspire them to obey.
> Oh may all who come behind us find us faithful."

In fact, isn't that what being part of a community of faith is all about? As we gather together, study the Word of God, and share our experiences with one another, we give and receive inspiration, challenging one another to greater heights of faith.

Take heart in the testimonies of those who have gone before, letting their victories carry you through your challenges. Then live your life as a testimony to those who will follow, becoming a part of that "great cloud of witnesses."

Find Us Faithful. Words and Music by Jon Mohr.
© 1988 Birdwing Music/Jonathan Mark Music
(admin. By The Sparrow Corp.)
All Rights Reserved. International Copyright secured.

Testimonies of the Ages

Drawing of the "Fortitude," Carried 256 immigrants. Held by John Oxley Library, State Library of Queensland.

European immigrants on deck. Photo courtesy of the Statue of Liberty-Ellis Island Foundation, Inc.

Carry On

Don't forget the stuff you come from,
souls who trekked across the seas,
hardy folks who sought to find
a better way, a life that's free.

Over ocean's depths and struggles
those who lived before you sailed,
hoping that what was before them
for their future would avail.

Never stop believing for the
future that they hoped you'd know.
Place one foot before the other;
Walk and see that faith can grow.

Always seek the heritage you
have from those who went before:
strength to be the man you want to,
hope for wings so you can soar.

Living spirits gather round to
watch o'er you and bid you peace,
call you onward, always upward,
to the vict'ry that faith brings.

Don the mantle and the armor;
stand where those before you stood,
in God's stead and with God's people,
seeking always for the good.

© 2005

Written for my husband's birthday. The first letters of each stanza form an acrostic of his name.

Freedom Isn't Free

We live in a country with the freedom to speak, freedom to worship, and freedom to achieve. Unfortunately, we sometimes forget that these freedoms came to us at a cost. Thousands of soldiers, sailors, politicians, activists, and even ordinary citizens fought to win that freedom for us. My own family was greatly impacted by World War II. Dad received a medical discharge, his brother Mike was killed at Okinawa, and on the other side of the family Uncle Andy received a purple heart for his injuries. This story is repeated many times over in every war that has been fought, both in this country and on foreign soil.

In is important to remember that our freedoms have come to us by someone else's sacrifice, because someone else stood up for what was right when many others wouldn't bother or couldn't come through. We need to remember our heroes, those who have taken the extra step, walked the extra mile, made the ultimate sacrifice.

> "Remember that you were slaves in Egypt and that the Lord your God brought you out of there with a mighty hand and an outstretched arm." (Deuteronomy 5:15a).

> "'Then you crossed the Jordan and came to Jericho. . . . You did not do it with your own sword and bow. So I gave you a land on which you did not toil and cities you did not build; and you live in them and eat from vineyards and olive groves that you did not plant" (Joshua 24:11-13).

When they arrived in the Promised Land, the Israelites were instructed, repeatedly, to remember that what they had was by God's grace and by God's hand. And so it is with the freedom we received when we put our faith in Jesus. We cannot live the Christian life without a constant reminder of this fact. It is part and parcel of who we are as children of God. Through Jesus' death on the cross, we have received the way to freedom from sin and separation from God, with no payment of our own. We receive that freedom by recognizing Jesus' life, death, and resurrection, by believing in faith.

> "He himself bore our sins in his body on the cross, so that we might die to sins and live for righteousness; "by his wounds you have been healed." (1 Peter 2:24).

Knowing who has paid the price makes us grateful, and being grateful, we are able to make a difference for others.

> "You were bought at a price. Therefore honor God with your body" (1 Corinthians 6:20).

Freedom comes at a price, a price that others have paid. Take the time to recognize those in your life and community who have given and continue to give so we might enjoy freedom and safety.

And in the spiritual realm, take some time to meditate on the offer of freedom purchased by Jesus' sacrifice on the cross. Thank God for setting you free from sin and giving you new life, then choose to live that life demonstrating your gratefulness and paying forward the grace you have received.

By the way, if you haven't accepted the offer of salvation and renewal, why not pray today, confessing your sins and professing your faith in Jesus? When you do, you'll find a freedom you never knew existed! Believe and be thankful!

> "Now the Lord is the Spirit, and where the Spirit of the Lord is, there is freedom" (2 Corinthians 3:17).

> "You, my brothers, were called to be free. But do not use your freedom to indulge the sinful nature; rather, serve one another in love" Galatians 5:13.

൯൰

Testimonies of the Ages

"Freedom Isn't Free" Collage

I Remember You

When I walk into my church, free and without fear,
I remember you.

When I see children playing in the school yard,
girls and boys from every place,
I remember you.

When I see families working together,
regardless of religion or nationality,
I remember you.

When I go to sleep
without worry for my family's safety,
I remember you.

When I see our flag waving in front of my home,
and when I can salute that flag without fear of reprisal,
I remember you.

When I remember you,
I think of the sacrifices you made
so I could have these things.
I think of your commitment and
your service beyond mere duty.

I think of all that you have given
so that I and those whom I love can be free.

When I pray at night and give thanks
for the blessings God has given,

I remember you.

©2004

The original inspiration for this poem was my father, who served in the U.S. Army during World War II and received a medical discharge after landing at Anzio, Italy. Although he is gone, I still remember and thank God for his service and that of all who have sacrificed for our freedoms.

Hands of Love

It was the strangest experience. Standing at the altar with Don, as our pastor served us from the Lord's Table, I was excited to finally be getting married, and to a great guy at that! I looked down and noticed the plain gold band I had just placed on his suntanned left hand, and in that moment I was taken back to another hand and another golden band.

My father's parents emigrated from Calabria, Italy, and dark olive skin and black curly hair were two of his identifying visual characteristics. As far back as I can remember, on Dad's left hand there was a simple golden band, a symbol of his love for and commitment to my mother. Through fifty-plus years of marriage he wore that ring, taking it off only when it was necessary to do so.

I can testify to the works of my father's hands, because I was there to witness many of them, and I know of many other deeds from the testimony of others. Dad left his home in the country so mom could be near her family in the city. Dad was always there when an elderly neighbor or one of my aunts needed help. He worked hard to support us and used his hands to repair and renovate our home.

One of my dearest memories of Dad is seeing him hold a baby. Those strong, dark hands with the golden ring held babies with strength and tenderness. He serenaded them with his repertoire of gospel, Nat King Cole, and Dean Martin. Each time I heard him sing I remembered how he sang to me when I was small. Hearing his voice let me know that everything would be okay. I will always cherish the memory of Dad holding and singing to each of my children.

The golden ring not only reminds me of my father's hands and character, but of my God's strong hands as well. I have witnessed numerous acts of mercy and love in my life and the lives of others, all from the hand of God. While spending time with a family grieving the loss of a loved one, I have sensed God's gentle hands surround them with the Spirit's comfort and strength. At the bedside of an ill child I have seen God's hands bring healing. And in my day-to-day struggles I have sensed God's hands holding me up when I feel like falling to my knees. And when I am struggling to believe, I see something—a ring, a rainbow, a picture of someone dear, a baby—that reminds me of the strong hands in which I rest, the hands of God.

When Dad was in the hospital and unresponsive, my brother sat and talked with him, and my sisters and I sang to him. Dad couldn't wear his ring any longer; the ring was too big and his hands much too thin. Seven days before their fifty-eighth anniversary, Dad passed from this life to the waiting arms of Jesus and was reunited with my mom in heaven. I have his ring, along with Mom's rings, in my jewelry case, a constant reminder of my father's love and of my heavenly Father who loves and cares for me even more.

> "Shout for joy, O heavens; rejoice, O earth; burst into song, O mountains! For the LORD comforts his people and will have compassion on his afflicted ones. But Zion said, "The LORD has forsaken me, the Lord has forgotten me."
> "Can a mother forget the baby at her breast and have no compassion on the child she has borne? Though she may forget, I will not forget you! See, I have engraved you on the palms of my hands; your walls are ever before me." (Isaiah 14:13-16)

> And the God of all grace, who called you to his eternal glory in Christ, after you have suffered a little while, will himself restore you and make you strong, firm and steadfast (1 Peter 5:10).

The Golden Ring

Dark and lovely, full of strength,
my father's solid hands.
on fingers long and slender shines
a simple golden band.

The ring was shining when Dad held
his little baby girl.
It shone when I was toddling,
And learned to dance and twirl.

I watched Dad as he built and worked
around the house and yard,
and when those hands reached out to help
the elderly and scarred.

The symbol of his love so deep
for my mother dear,
the golden ring was shining bright
with love throughout the years.

My wedding day had come and gone
and as we honeymooned,
there I glimpsed my husband's hand
with golden band festooned.

Representing vows we made
to love and faithful be,
that shiny, simple golden band
brought Dad's love back to me.

Now Dad's hands are thin and weak.
His years are winding down.
The ring's too big to stay in place,
And Mom, his love, is gone.

Words of Wisdom . . . Thoughts of Hope

*Yet when I look at Daddy's hands
and take his hands in mine,
e'en without the golden band
his love and strength still shines.*

© 2006

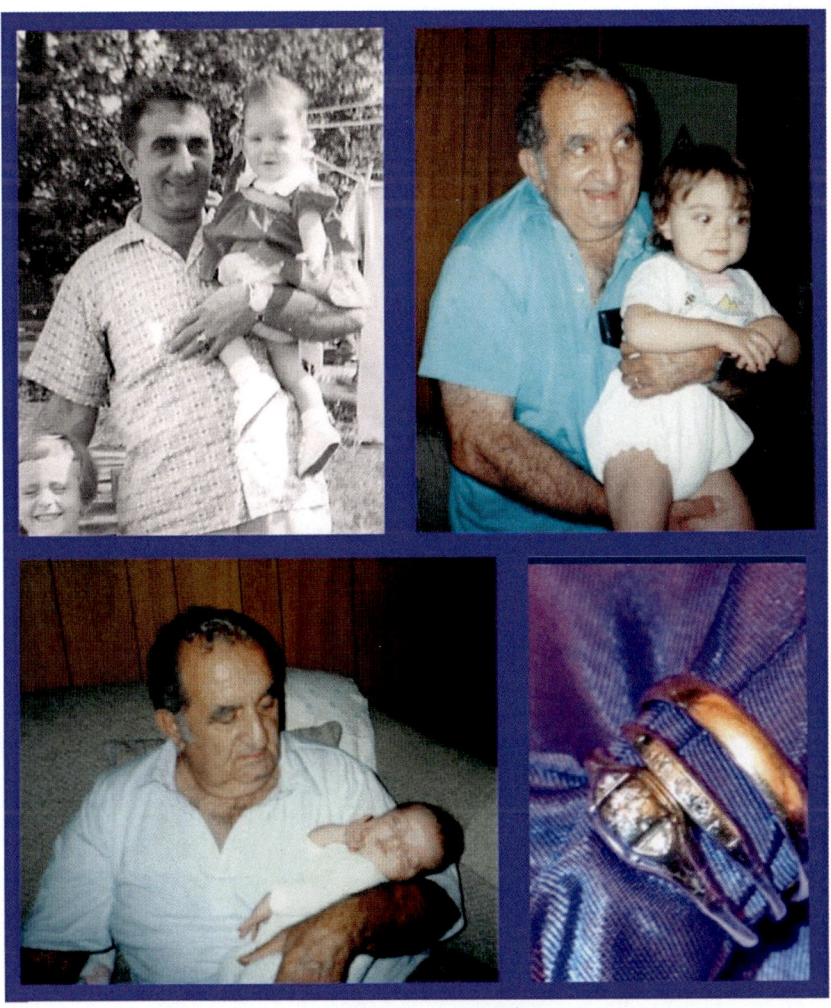

My Dad, Domenick "Mickey" Caristo
August 17, 1924 – January 22, 2007
We miss you, too, Dad!

Generation to Generation

  Living close to a thousand miles from my parents, my children missed many of the blessings I had in my childhood. Growing up in a second-generation American family, I had numerous aunts, uncles, cousins, near cousins, and people who might as well have been related because our families were so close.

  Through the alley-way between the houses, by the small courtyard, was my grandparents' three-story Victorian-era building. Baba (my Slovak grandmother) lived in the first-floor apartment. I would run over there to watch her cook, to pet her dog, to listen to her talk on the phone in Slovak, and to eat her homemade noodles. Her home was a treasure trove of exploration and imagination. But with all the opportunities for imagination in my grandmother's house, one thing didn't require imagination—her love for her children and for every one of her grandchildren.

  One night, when I was a teenager, Baba decided to talk to me about growing up issues—makeup, boys, etc. Born a poor farm girl in a small village in Slovakia, Baba had a different view of things.

  "Mary Kay," she said with her Old World accent, "not to worry about things like making up your face and fancy clothes, and boys all the time." (As if that was ever a problem I had!) "When man looks for wife, he wants woman strong, like bull, so she can carry water from the well." Laughing on the inside, I reminded her that we have running water and don't need to carry it anymore. She wasn't deterred. "Mary Kay, I pray for you, that you find good Christian man one day, man who love God!"

  I couldn't take it any longer; I started to laugh out loud. All I could picture was a guy who would drag me to church every day. No way! Not me! Once a week was plenty!

Strange as it may seem, my life today is a testimony to a grandmother's prayers as I am married to a man who, as I do, serves God in full-time ministry! I am grateful that God heard her prayers in spite of my lack of vision and faith.

Throughout the Bible the influence and testimony of the elders was an important part of life—sometimes for good and sometimes for bad, but always with result. One of the most telling examples covers the space of one verse in Paul's second letter to Timothy. "I have been reminded of your sincere faith, which first lived in your grandmother Lois and in your mother Eunice and, I am persuaded, now lives in you also" (2 Timothy 1:5).

Although we are responsible for our own faith, it rarely begins just with us. It comes down from those in whom it first lived, whether related by blood or simple relationships, inspiring the flame in our own hearts. From there, we can't help but pass on the flame to those who come after us. I'm sure Timothy thought many times about his grandmother Lois and his mother Eunice, and thanked God for their examples.

In many ways "Baba" was God's hand extended to me. She wasn't perfect, and wasn't always even-tempered, but she was faithful and full of faith in God. My prayer is that one day my children and grandchildren will look back to their youth and remember the "sincere faith that first lived in your grandmother and your mother" and testify to that sincere faith that then lives in their hearts.

ೞ౸

The Angel in my Grandma's House

*Room dark and looming with antiques around,
ceilings much higher than I'd ever touch,
dark heavy curtains that kept out the cold and
overstuffed chairs that snuggled so much.*

*There in the room where my grandma was sitting
I learned about love and I learned about doubt.
But the greatest discovery there in the shadows
was finding the angel in my Grandma's house.*

*There on the wall, right next to my uncle,
where portraits of all in the family were hung,
In a huge frame with gold scrolls all around it
A picture of children—one older, one young.*

*The baby was sleeping, the sister was sitting
And knitting a scarf to shield from the cold.
I wondered why Mama was not in the room there
with arms snug and warm her baby to hold.*

*There in the dim room, shining and strong,
an angel looked over the children at rest,
recording their stories and names in his book,
guarding and keeping them safe, warm, and blest.*

*Long years have passed and my grandma's in heaven;
the angel now shines from a frame in my room.
And as I remember the strong, shining angel
I rewrite the stories that once used to bloom.*

*See, Grandma would watch me when Mama was busy.
She helped me know Jesus and taught me to pray.
My Grandma was there when my baby teeth loosened.
She taught me to make lots of good food her way.*

*She made sure I knew that my Mom and Dad loved me
and always had snacks for me there on her shelf.
You see, the real angel there in that room
Was not in the frame, but was Grandma herself.*

*Based on this print that really did
hang in my grandmother's living room.*

On the Way Home

Chapter 5

On the Way Home

The Beauty of Adoption

A few years before I was born, five to be exact, a baby boy came to live with my parents. My aunt, in the midst of a divorce, realized she was unable to care for this four-month-old bundle and asked my parents to care for him. It was a tremendous answer to Mom's prayers, as she had been told she could not have children. She jumped into motherhood, even if it was not a child she had carried. A few years later they started adoption proceedings for a baby girl, whom they named Mary Katherine, but this was short-lived, as her parents ended the adoption proceedings and took my big sister back home.

Through the following years, although God was faithful and allowed my "barren" mother to bear three girls, Frank was nothing less than a full-fledged son to them and brother to us. Yes, his birth mother was involved in our lives, and when people asked why my brother had a different last name, I'd just answer "I don't know" and move on.

During those years our parents often asked for permission to adopt Frank legally, but his birth mom steadfastly refused, even though his birth father had long-since rescinded any relationship. Even without a legal ruling testifying that Frank was theirs, Mom and Dad continued to raise "their son" and my big brother as their own.

Frank had changed his last name to match ours when he turned 21 so that he was a "Caristo" legally. Fast forward almost 30 years. My parents decided to finally make the relationship official. Mom and Dad hired an attorney to represent them, and they went to court to formally adopt Frank as their legal heir at the age of 48.

The judge didn't quite know how to proceed, as he had never officiated at such an adoption before. Members of each side of our family were there. Each parent testified as to why they began the proceedings, and Frank testified how he had always been a son in this household. By the end of the session everyone was in tears and Frank was **legally** our brother. He had finally been adopted.

The beauty of adoption is that a child, without parents for whatever reason, is chosen to become part of a family. Most often this child brings nothing to the relationship except being there. The adoptive parents reach out to this lost young one, offering to provide nurture, sustenance, and love to help the child grow.

We were lost at one time, separated from God our Creator, the original Parent of all, because of sin. We had no way to change the relationship on our own because we had nothing to bring to God, nothing that would make us worthy of being in God's presence.

Yet, even in our lost condition, God saw something more than this world could ever see. Because of God's love for us, Jesus Christ suffered and died to pay the price for our adoption, to redeem us from sin and bring us into the family of God when we believe in faith. This adoption takes away any stigma from our past life, making us new and complete, and giving us a new family where we once were alone.

The beauty of adoption is being chosen, being wanted, and becoming a part of family. I'm glad to have an older brother, in heart and in law, and as the song says, "I'm so glad I'm a part of the family of God."*

> Praise be to the God and Father of our Lord Jesus Christ, who has blessed us in the heavenly realms with every spiritual blessing in Christ. For he chose us in him before the creation of the world to be holy and blameless in his sight. In love he predestined us for adoption to sonship through Jesus Christ, in accordance with his pleasure and will—to the praise of his glorious grace, which he has freely given us in the One he loves. (Ephesians 1:3-5).

*The Family of God, By William J. & Gloria Gaither,
© 1970, William J. Gaither, Inc.

Just as a father
has compassion on
his children,
so the Lord
has compassion
on those who fear Him.
For He Himself
knows our frame;
He is mindful
that we are but dust.

Psalm 103:13-14

From the Father's Heart

*Precious child with heart of love
and tiny arms stretched up to gain
a glimpse of joy, a look of trust,
a tender hug to ease your pain.*

*The days of childhood now long past,
yet still the deepest hope remains
that father dear will take you up
in loving arms with no disdain.*

*You know how much your Father loved
and sent His Son so you could be
a child of God, adopted in,
beloved in Christ and from sin freed.*

*And in the nights of dark and fear,
reach out to me and call my name.
Keep your eyes turned heavenward;
I saw your start, I made your frame.*

*Every day remember, child, that
once for you Christ died and rose,
So call on me, I'll hear your voice,
for you're the daughter that I chose.*

© 2005

*Poem written for my late friend Patty after the death of her father.
His affectionate name for her was "Pattycakes."
The poem base is actually an acronym of that nickname.*

Help for the Weary

When the Israelites found themselves at war with the Amalekites, Moses went to the top of the hill and held up his staff. As long as Moses' hands were up, the Israelites were winning the battle. However, when Moses' arms became tired, the Israelites started to lose. Exodus 17 tells us that the Israelites did, indeed, win the battle, but not without help.

> When Moses' hands grew tired, they took a stone and put it under him and he sat on it. Aaron and Hur held his hands up—one on one side, one on the other—so that his hands remained steady till sunset. (Exodus 17:12).

No matter what the situation, there are few people who are always strong, always filled with faith, always able to stand. We struggle and we want to be faithful, but we often weaken, whether emotionally, physically, or spiritually, and need the help of others. The one who says he is strong and has no need of help is a fool and is filled with pride. We all know the proverb: "Pride goes before destruction, a haughty spirit before a fall" (Proverbs 16:18). Thinking that we are able to do everything for ourselves will cause us to trip and make mistakes. When we depend on one another, however, that is when we are strong.

We are not made to walk, to work, or to carry all of our burdens alone. God saw that "it was not good for man to be alone" and created Eve to be Adam's companion (Genesis 2:18-23). When Moses was wearied by judging the entire people of Israel in the wilderness, God send the Spirit upon the elders so they could help lead the people and give Moses some relief (Numbers 11). When Paul began his ministry, Barnabas took him under his wing, and they ministered together (Acts 9). Even Jesus, in the Garden of Gethsemane, asked his disciples to stay awake with him as He prayed (Matthew 26).

Have you ever wondered why geese honk at one another and fly in formation? Scientists tell us that when they fly in formation the air flow creates lift, helping those behind to fly with less effort. They honk at one another to communication and encourage one another, and if one falls behind, two others will leave the formation to be with the weak one and protect it until it regains its strength.

At some time in our lives we all need someone to help carry our burdens. In fact, the Bible commands us to do so. "Carry each other's burdens, and in this way you will fulfill the law of Christ" (Galatians 6:2). The book of James tells us to go to one another with our burdens.

> "Is anyone among you in trouble? Let them pray. Is anyone happy? Let them sing songs of praise. Is anyone among you sick? Let them call the elders of the church to pray over them and anoint them with oil in the name of the Lord. And the prayer offered in faith will make the sick person well; the Lord will raise them up. If they have sinned, they will be forgiven. Therefore confess your sins to each other and pray for each other so that you may be healed. The prayer of a righteous person is powerful and effective."
> (James 5:13-16)

Are you disappointed that you aren't able to stand alone? Do you feel like a failure because your faith isn't always as strong as you want it to be? You are no different than Moses, Paul, and even Jesus, who all asked for help from others. Lean on your brothers and sisters. Call on them for prayer and support. Do you have needs that you cannot overcome on your own? Enlist a trusted friend to pray with you and for you. You'll find yourself strong again soon, able to stand and be strong for those who need your help.

> "A friend loves at all times, and a brother is born for adversity" (Proverbs 17:17).

Thank You, Lord, for Wings

*On the ground the daily struggle,
on and on it bids me go.
Time to time and task to task
I soon see only more to do.*

*Once the joy of work accomplished,
now the tedious commonplace.
Once excitement in the journey,
now just tiredness in this space.*

*Where, O Lord, the joy of serving
just for heav'nly service's sake?
Where the faith that took me upward,
now just lukewarm, half awake?*

*Step by step I try to look to
where I once found purpose strong,
but my eyes again see only
more to do, no joyful song.*

*Then a voice calls to remind me
nothing's lost of what we do.
God brings beauty out of ashes;
simple deeds have value, too.*

*All alone I cannot make this
journey through the day to day,
so my friend holds out a hand
to help me find again my way.*

*Soon I'm flying up above
the ordinary and I see
there below a better view of
what the commonplace can mean.*

©

*Thank you, Lord, for wings that take me
up above what I can see,
there to see through heaven's eyes,
a vision to eternity.*

*And when those wings are having trouble
knowing how to soar above,
thank you for the friends who lift me
to the heavens by your love.*

© 2006

Geese Flying Past

Following the Shepherd

One of my favorite books is Hind's Feet on High Places, an allegory of the Christian faith. A young woman named Much Afraid, who lives in the Valley of Humiliation, wants to serve the Great Shepherd, but she is crippled and disfigured and fears she would never be accepted. Eventually, however, the Great Shepherd does call Much Afraid to join him on his way to the High Places, and her journey of faith begins.

I suppose the reason I love this book so much is that I identify with Much Afraid in many ways. Though not physically disfigured, I have often felt emotionally disfigured by relationships and by mistakes I have made. I also remember when, as a child, I really didn't understand the security of God's love and wondered what I needed to do for God to love and accept me.

Following the Great Shepherd wasn't easy for Much Afraid, as it isn't always easy for us. God leads us through paths that we don't understand and sometimes appears to be absent when we need Him most. We get angry and afraid. We doubt God's love for us and sometimes even turn back to our old lives and relationships to try to find comfort and what seems like stability.

The truth about the journey, however, is that we are never on our own, even when it feels that way. Like a parent helping a child walk, even when God lets go of our hands, God is always nearby to catch us when we toddle and fall. And when the journey goes in a direction we don't understand—or don't like—God is able to make each step of the journey into something meaningful, to weave it into something that brings good (Romans 8:28). Some experiences strengthen us. Some change our way of thinking. While others may just be necessary for us to reach the High Places of faith.

Are you like Much Afraid, wondering where God is taking you and why God has led you to where you are?

Are you like Much Afraid, wondering where God is taking you and why God has led you to where you are? Are you wondering if God truly does care for you? Many people in the Bible were in the same position when their circumstances seemed to be devastating. They had to choose whether to give up or to continue to trust God.

Proverbs offers counsel for the times when we find ourselves feeling lost or confused about God's plan.

*"Trust in the Lord with all your heart
and lean not on your own understanding;
in all your ways submit to him,
and he will make your paths straight."
(Proverbs 3:5-6)*

King David went through many times of loss and persecution, but when we read the Psalms, we find advice for the times when we are questioning God's plans and direction.

*"Commit your way to the Lord;
trust in him and he will do this:
He will make your righteous reward
shine like the dawn, your vindication
like the noonday sun." (Psalm 37:5-6).*

At each step in the journey Much Afraid had to choose whether to continue her journey to the High Places, trusting in the Shepherd in spite of what her rational mind told her, or to turn back to her former life. I won't tell you what happened; I'll let you read it for yourself. I can tell you this: God is always faithful and will always lead us home.

Additional reading: Check out <u>Hind's Feet on High Places</u> by Hannah Hurnard, and the sequel, <u>Mountains of Spices</u>

ଔଓ

"The Good Shepherd"
by Zeger Jacob van Helmont
(public domain)

Shepherd's Song

My sheep, they know my voice,
they hear me when I speak.
And when I lead they follow
through paths both bright and bleak.

Don't think they're always happy
or always doing great.
Even sheep get lonely
or frightened or irate.

Look up above when you can't see
beyond the deepest night.
If that darkness hides your way,
remember, I'm your Light.

New challenges will come, it's true,
but you are not alone.
Even if you doubt the way
I will lead you home.

*Written for a young girl's birthday
as she was battling leukemia*

On the Journey

I have lived away from my hometown for over two decades. This was no small feat, as I was close to my family and friends. The adjustment to living in another state was a great one, but it was tempered by my husband's presence. Together we experienced the journey, through college, seminary, children, etc., carrying one another through life's journey here in the Midwest.

Likewise, living in a college town has had its blessings and its sorrows. We met many good friends through the years, only to have them move on to other callings, other locales, to carry on the will of God in their lives. In each case our lives were nourished by the times we had together, and each time the separation brought pain as our lives were changed once again.

No matter what relationships we find here on earth, they are all temporal, short-lived compared to the eternity we will spend together with those whom we know as brothers and sisters in Christ. We look forward to the day when there will be no more good-byes and no more separation, but until then we must carry on.

Some years ago my children met a friend in youth group named Bryan. An affable young man, he was a good friend, always ready to laugh, and committed to Christ. The three of them became best friends and spent their time, when they weren't in church, playing video games, sledding, texting on their cell phones or online, and playing in the church yard. As a parent, knowing my kids had such a great friend was an answer to prayer.

All of that changed abruptly one day in May 2010 when, at a community gathering, Bryan collapsed because of a formerly undiagnosed heart condition, and 15-year-old Bryan Wallace passed from this life to eternity.

At the memorial service, several individuals shared what Bryan's short life had meant to them. Then a youth leader shared a letter Bryan wrote the morning before he died. Bryan talked about how God changed his life and how important his faith had become. He expressed his intent to follow God into the future, whatever it brings.

Listening to Brian's letter, we were in awe of what God had done in his heart, and years later, we are in awe when we recognize how Bryan's testimony, even in death, continues to spur others on to faith and dedication to the Lord.

It is hard to grieve for one's own losses, but to watch your children grieve is a terrible challenge. We shared many tears, but it was a valley, a dark valley, that they had to tread, trying to understand how a life could be so-soon lost in the will of God. The youth took comfort in knowing that they could trust God even though they didn't understand God's plan. This is God's promise: "The LORD is close to the brokenhearted and saves those who are crushed in spirit" (Psalm 34:18).

We all will, if we have not yet, find ourselves in times of sorrow and loss. The pain of loss may be great, and it will take time to recover and get back on the road toward heaven, but we are not alone on that road. There are many others on the journey to heaven. Although we find ourselves in sorrow, when we look up from our tears, from our pain, we will see them, individuals who themselves have found their way through grief and pain, and we will be able to continue on, strengthened by their testimony and building relationships once again, until it is our turn to cross over to glory and eternity.

> "Praise be to the God and Father of our Lord Jesus Christ, the Father of compassion and the God of all comfort, who comforts us in all our troubles, so that we can comfort those in any trouble with the comfort we ourselves receive from God" (2 Corinthians 1:3-4).

Emmanuel's Land Window
at Emmanuel Church in the City of Boston
(depicting Bunyan's Pilgrim's Progress.

Home!

Home! What a warming thought!
  Visions of loved ones,
      open arms,
          warm smiles,
              reunion.

Away for such a long time,
the heart of the traveler longs for home.

Weary days are forgotten when home is in sight.
The glories of heaven and of home outshine,
even block out, the struggles and the weariness
of the journey now ended.

Joyful reunion!
  Glorious day!
      When Jesus greets those
          who have joined Him at home.

But those who still travel must be content
to look for the day when their journey will end.
The space on the road
where the home-gone traveler had been
now seems empty, lonely.

Those who remain rejoice at the thought
of the reunion their friend has found,
yet they ache at the loss of the hand they held,
  of the smile that cheered,
      of the heart that encouraged.

The sweetness of their memories
and the hope of their own homegoing
    will bring healing and,
        after a short time of rest,
            the travelers will once again
                stand and continue the journey.

Seeing another weary traveler,
  they begin to speak of home
      and of the One who waits.

Home! What a warming thought!

© 1988

List of Illustrations

Page 4
Princess straightening her crown. This photo is all over the internet, and although I made every effort to find the owner, I haven't been able. May be subject to copyright.

Page 8
"In the Hand of God." http://www.grace2help.com/2012/11/24/week-twentythe-hand-of-god/

Page 13
Chimes and butterfly in the trees. Photo by Mary Kay Glunt, 2016. This picture incorporates jewelry I inherited from my mother, a butterfly prism ornament given to me by a dear friend, and several wind chimes that play beautiful music.

Page 18
"Solitude." Don Glunt © 2016. Used with permission.

Page 22
"Sea Beside Seashore." Sabri Ismail. Creative Commons Zero (CC0) license.

Page 26
"In His Constant Care." Simon Dewey. Used by permission Altus Fine Art/www.altusfineart.com.

Page 30
Caristo Family Photos

Page 34
"His Eye Is On the Sparrow" Chalk Art. Cindi Koeich, To Such as These Designs at ToSuchAsTheseDesigns.etsy.com.

Page 41
Burning candle (reflection added). CC0 Public Domain. https://pixabay.com/en/candlelight-candle-light-1077638/

Page 44
Caristo Family Photo

Steven Curtis Chapman quote. http://quoteestate.com/quotes/16133

Page 49
"Kindergarten." Hugo Oehmichen. Public Domain, https://commons.wikimedia.org/w/index.php?curid=434096. This work is in the public domain in its country of origin and in the United States as copyright expired.

Page 54
Fortitude (ship). "Drawing of the 'Fortitude." Item is held by John Oxley Library, State Library of Queensland.

Photo of European immigrants on way to America. Photo courtesy of the Statue of Liberty-Ellis Island Foundation, Inc.; "From the Pale to the Golden Land: Journey by Sea: Voyage of Opportunity." http://www.museumoffamilyhistory.com/mfh-imm-jbs.htm,

Page 58
"Freedom Isn't Free" Collage, consisting of:
Center: Flag in front of house. Mary Kay Glunt 2002

Upper Left: Michael Caristo, family photo

Top Right: 10th Mountain Medic treats Afghan boy via https://creativecommons.org/licenses/by/2.0

Center Right: "Tomb of the Unknown Soldier. U.S. Navy photo by Chief Warrant Officer Seth Rossman. [Public domain], via Wikimedia Commons.

Bottom Right: Vietnam – Treating Civilians. U.S. Navy BUMED Library and Archives. Public Domain. https://www.flickr.com/photos/medicalmuseum/4152214259/

Bottom Center: Purple Heart. Photo by Mary Kay Glunt.

Bottom Left: "Victim of Terror." Photo by Lance Cpl. James F. Cline III, March 27, 2007. Public Domain. A soldier carries a wounded Iraqi child into the Charlie Medical Center at Camp Ramadi, Iraq, March 20.

Page 63
Caristo Family Photos.

Page 67
Antique Victorian Angel Print. Public Domain.

List of Illustrations

Page 72
Glunt Family Photo.

Adult and child hands. Creative Commons Zero (CC0) license. Source: unsplash.com https://www.pexels.com/photo/hands-carrying-child-father-27118/

Page 77
"Geese Flying Past." Uploaded by Magnus Manske, Author. https://upload.wikimedia.org/wikipedia/commons/a/a5/Geese_Flying_Past_(635 3898479).jpg

Page 80
"The Good Shepherd," By Zeger Jacob van Helmont. Public domain, copyright expired. https://commons.wikimedia.org/wiki/File:Zeger_Jacob_van_Helmont_-_The_Good_Shepherd.jpg

Page 84
Emmanuel's Land Window at Emmanuel Church in the City of Boston (depicting Bunyan's Pilgrim's Progress. Designed by Frederic Crowninshield [1845-1918].) By ElizaJR (Own work) [Public domain], via Wikimedia Commons.

☙❧

Made in the USA
Middletown, DE
12 March 2024